George Winston
PIANO SOLOS

Exact Transcriptions From The Recordings
Authorized by **GEORGE WINSTON**

ISBN-13: 978-1-4234-1709-5
ISBN-10: 1-4234-1709-7

7777 W. BLUEMOUND RD. P.O. BOX 13819 MILWAUKEE, WI 53213

Visit Hal Leonard Online at
www.halleonard.com

NOTES FROM GEORGE WINSTON

These are exact transcriptions of 20 songs from my albums, with chord labels included. One should feel free to interpret and change them however they want—I do that with all songs that I play. (These transcribed versions are just the way the songs were played on the days that I recorded them). I learn music by ear, and I use chords and music theory to learn and remember music (see facing page).

One of the reasons I play the piano is that I prefer the quality of the sustain that the piano has over strings or organ, etc. I often use the sustain pedal for extended time periods, so sometimes some of the notes will sound like they are struck—but what is actually happening is that when the pedal is held down for awhile, the overtones will sometimes swell and sound like a softly struck note. In this book these types of sustained notes are indicated with a tie. You could strike those notes if you prefer to.

The other reason I play the piano is because it has power and volume, and because it is possible to play a lot of songs with multiple parts as solo instrumentals, which is my temperament as a musician. I mainly think of the piano as if it is an Afro-American tuned drum.

Many thanks to Tom Bockhold (www.tombockhold.com) for doing the initial transcriptions that I later fine-tuned while listening to the recordings, and for being so great to work with, and for understanding so well my unusual ways of playing.

WHETHER YOU LEARN music by ear or from the written page, I suggest learning chords (any combination of three notes or more played together) and music theory (how chords are used in the different music traditions). Any piece of written music could be analyzed in terms of its chord structures, and that can be an aid in memorization. The individual notes are like the letters in the alphabet, and chords are like words. The Major and minor chords are the building blocks for all other chords. Here is a suggested way to learn chords:

1. First learn the Major chords, which have the 1st, 3rd, and 5th notes of the Major scale of a key.
2. Then learn the minor chords, which have the 3rd lowered a half step (down one note).
3. The next step would be to learn the dominant 7th chords, the minor 7th chords, and the Major 7th chords.
4. Then learn the 9th chords (adding the 9th note with those three types of 7th chords mentioned just above in #3).
5. Then learn the diminished chords (and the diminished 7th chords), and the augmented chords.
6. Then learn the Major 6th and the minor 6th chords.
7. And then, if it is an area one is interested in, learn the jazz chords—13th chords, flat 9th chords, augmented 9th chords, flat 5 chords, 11th chords, and more; and also scales and modes.

Again, any combination of three notes or more can be called a chord (and actually any chord could be interpreted in twelve different ways, depending on its use in any of the twelve keys).

Here are the Major and minor chords:

KEY	MAJOR	MINOR
C	C-E-G	C-E♭-G
D♭	D♭-F-G♭	D♭-E-G♭
D	D-F♯-A	D-F-A
E♭	E♭-G-B♭	E♭-G♭-B♭
E	E-G♯-B	E-G-B
F	F-A-C	F-A♭-C
G♭	G♭-B♭-D♭	G♭-A-D♭
G	G-B-D	G-B♭-D
A♭	A♭-C-E♭	Ab-B-Eb
A	A-C♯-E	A-C-E
B♭	B♭-D-F	B♭-D♭-F
B	B-D♯-F♯	B-D-F♯

A great book for exploring more about chords is **Picture Chord Encyclopedia for Keyboard** (HL00290528). This book has photos, diagrams, and music notation for over 1,600 keyboard chords. See **www.halleonard.com**.

Some other recommended books from Hal Leonard (see **www.halleonard.com**):

The Vince Guaraldi Collection (HL00672486) has the most accurate transcription of Vince's song *Linus and Lucy* available. It also has Vince's *Cast Your Fate to the Wind*, *Christmas Time Is Here*, and Vince's wonderful arrangement of *Greensleeves*, and five other songs.

The Peanuts Illustrated Songbook (HL00313178) has a nice introduction by Hank Bordowitz and 30 of Vince's Peanuts® pieces including *Skating*, *The Great Pumpkin Waltz*, *Christmas Is Coming*, *Christmas Time Is Here*, and many more.

Philip Aaberg, the great Montana pianist and composer, who is the only melodic pianist whose work I have studied, has a book **Philip Aaberg Piano Solos** (HL00308262), with 13 songs.

Three Ghost Rags (HL00009638) includes the original sheet music for the song *Graceful Ghost* by composer/pianist William Bolcom. (I rearranged and recorded a shorter version of *Graceful Ghost* on my album FOREST).

Guitarist Ed Wright has transcribed 10 of George's songs for the book **George Winston for Solo Guitar** (HL00306822).

SONG NOTES

THE BLACK STALLION
By the late composer Carmine Coppola from the 1979 film of the same name.

THE CRADLE
By the late jazz organist Larry Young (Khalid Yasim), composed for just organ and drums, from his 1968 album HEAVEN ON EARTH. Dedicated to moms everywhere.

GRADUATION
Inspired by the Spring season and Eastern Montana.

JOY
By J.S. Bach, originally titled *Jesus, Joy of Man's Desiring*, and inspired by an arrangement by the great guitarist David Qualey from his album GUITAR SOLO (Telefunken Records 6.23413 – German import).
www.david-qualey.de/index.html

LORETA AND DESIREE'S BOUQUET – PART 1
Inspired by two friends of mine.

LONGING/LOVE
A song inspired by the Autumn season.

LULLABY
The epilogue is taken from the song *Gypsy Hollow* by the great pianist and composer Steve Ferguson (also see his albums THE WELL TEMPERED PIANO – VOLUMES 1 & 2). **www.stevefergusonmusic.com**

NEW HOPE BLUES
Inspired by the great stride pianist Thomas "Fats" Waller (1904-1943), especially his solo and band recordings between 1929 and 1936; and by the great solo blues/ragtime guitarist Blind Blake, who recorded prolifically in the 1920s. See **www.redhotjazz.com/fat** and **www.georgewinston.com/faqs.html#fats**

PRELUDE/CAROL OF THE BELLS
Prelude was inspired by the late jazz pianist and composer Vince Guaraldi (1928-1976). Vince Guaraldi was best known for his standard piece *Cast Your Fate to the Wind* from 1962, and for his soundtracks for the first 16 Peanuts® animations, starting with A CHARLIE BROWN CHRISTMAS (Fantasy Records) in 1965, until he passed on in 1976. I recorded an album of his compositions, LINUS & LUCY – THE MUSIC OF VINCE GUARALDI, in 1996, and a second volume is planned.

Carol of the Bells is a traditional Ukrainian Winter song. This version was inspired by my childhood Winters in Billings, Montana.

REFLECTION
A song inspired by early Spring.

STEVENSON
Dedicated to my dear late friend, New Orleans filmmaker Stevenson J. Palfi (1952-2005), who made the wonderful film **Piano Players Rarely Ever Play Together** about the New Orleans pianists Professor Longhair, Allen Toussaint, and Isidore "Tuts" Washington. Stevenson Palfi also produced the film **Setting the Record Straight** about the late violinist Papa John Creach, and the upcoming documentary release **Songwriter, Unknown** about the New Orleans composer/pianist Allen Toussaint.

THANKSGIVING
Inspired by friends and places of Miles City, Montana.

THUMBELINA
From Mark Isham's score for the Rabbit Ears Productions video and soundtrack recording of the classic children's story **Thumbelina**. I am also inspired by his soundtracks for their production of the children's stories **The Steadfast Tin Soldier** and **The Emperor and the Nightingale**. The music from these three stories has been released as soundtracks with narration; and the music alone has also been released on his album SONGS MY CHILDREN TAUGHT ME. **www.isham.com**

THE TWISTING OF THE HAY ROPE

I play this traditional Irish piece as a spring love song. I first learned it from the American Celtic harpist Patrick Ball (www.patrickball.com) from his album FIONA, and was also inspired by the very soulful, slower version recorded by the Irish group the Bothy Band, with the Gaelic title *Casadh An tSúgáin* from their live album AFTER HOURS.

The title can be interpreted as having several deeper meanings: the binding of love and the intertwining of lives; strawings for traditional Irish wedding parties, where hay ropes were twisted and used for strawboys' costumes; in spring planting, where bundles of small plants were held together by a long rope of twisted straw; the many traditions of Ireland intertwining together to form Irish culture; and ornaments in traditional Irish music, beautifully twisting and turning around the melody notes.

This song was published in Edward Bunting's book from 1796, **A General Collection of the Ancient Irish Music**, which was reprinted in 2002 with his two other wonderful volumes from 1809 and 1840, with the title **The Ancient Music of Ireland–The Bunting Collection**, which includes almost 300 Irish melodies. (See **www.waltonsmusic.com/publications/collections.htm** and **www.clarsach.net/sourcebooks.htm**).

Thanks to Rick Epping for his help with this information.

(VARIATIONS ON) BAMBOO

A traditional Chinese lullaby, which I first learned in Taiwan, and is also known as *Bao Bei*, which can refer to a young child as a treasure. This arrangement was inspired by my dear friend Ling-Wen Tsai, and her deep and wonderful visual and performance art, and her friendship and guidance. **www.lingwentsai.com**

I have for decades been very inspired and influenced by many of the beautiful and incredibly expressive Chinese music traditions, particularly by the great players of the *gu-zheng* (pronounced "goo-jung"; sometimes spelled *guzheng*, *zheng*, or *cheng*), the Chinese zither/ harp with 16 to 25 strings and an adjustable bridge. It is the ancestor of the Japanese *koto*. I have been especially inspired by the playing of Wei-Shan Liu (**www.guzheng.org**), on her solo instrumental recordings THE MAGNIFICIENT BRONZE GORGE and MORNING BELL.

For an expanded version of these notes on Chinese classical and traditional music and more recommended websites, go to **www.georgewinston.com**, and see the FAQ section, and go to the question "How have you been inspired by Chinese traditional music and Chinese classical music?".

VARIATIONS ON THE KANON BY PACHELBEL

Composed circa 1699, the *Kanon* may have originated as a solo pipe organ piece.

THE VELVETEEN RABBIT

The main theme for the solo piano soundtrack I did for the video and audio production of the classic children's story written by Margery Williams in 1922, with accompanying narration by Meryl Streep.

WALKING IN THE AIR (abridged version) – FROM *THE SNOWMAN*

The main theme from the beautiful children's animation **The Snowman**, with orchestra music composed by Howard Blake (soundtrack on CBS FM Records). This transcription is an abridged version of the one I recorded on the FOREST album, reflecting just the main theme from **The Snowman** (leaving out the two other sections by two other composers in the version that I recorded on the FOREST album).

BUILDING THE SNOWMAN – FROM *THE SNOWMAN*

Another theme from the beautiful children's animation **The Snowman**, with orchestra music composed by Howard Blake.

THE SNOWMAN'S MUSIC BOX DANCE – FROM *THE SNOWMAN*

Another theme from the beautiful children's animation **The Snowman**, with orchestra music composed by Howard Blake.

THE BLACK STALLION

from the solo piano album SUMMER

By CARMINE COPPOLA
Arranged by George Winston

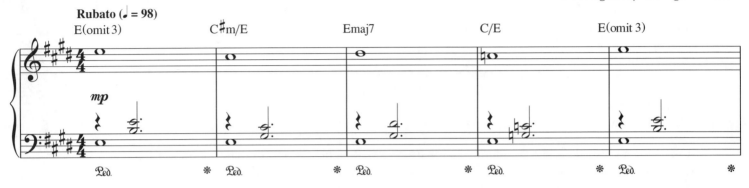

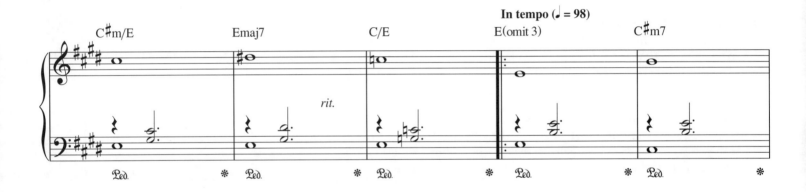

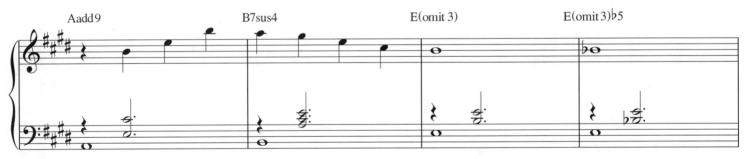

Pedal simile throughout

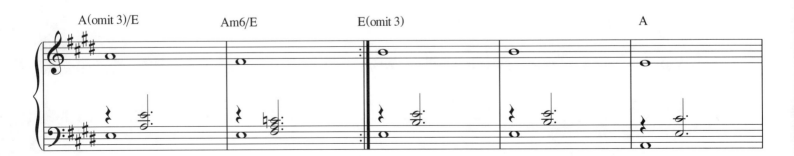

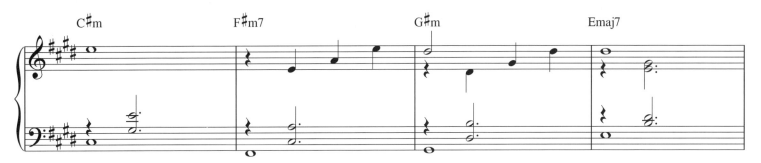

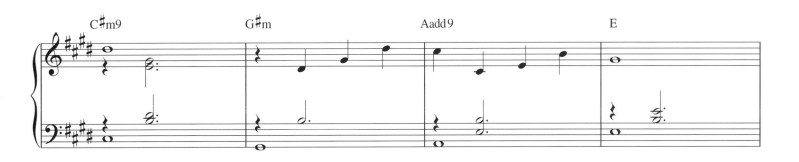

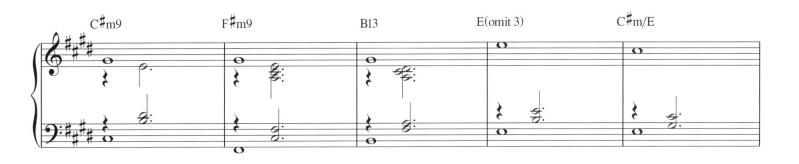

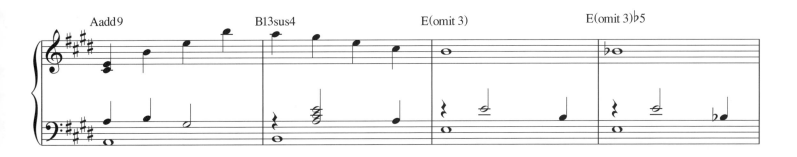

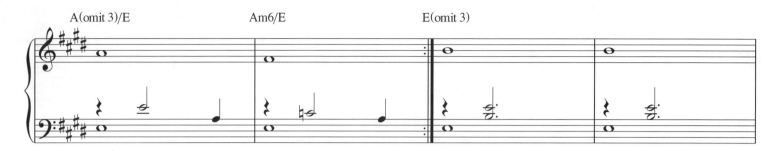

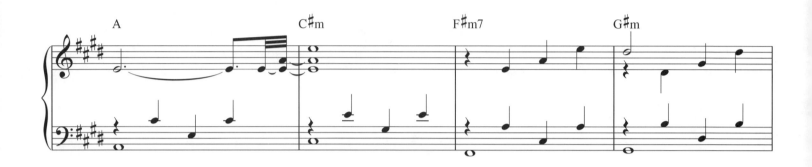

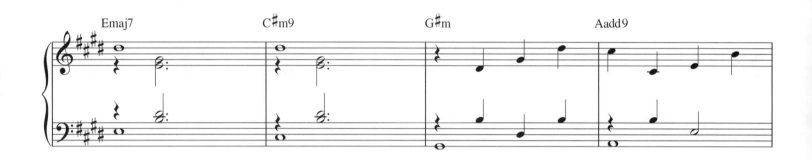

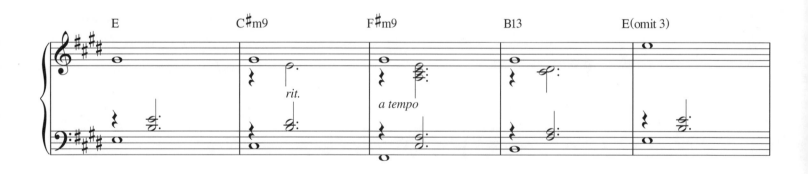

THE CRADLE
from the solo piano album FOREST

By LARRY YOUNG (KHALID YASIM)
Arranged by George Winston

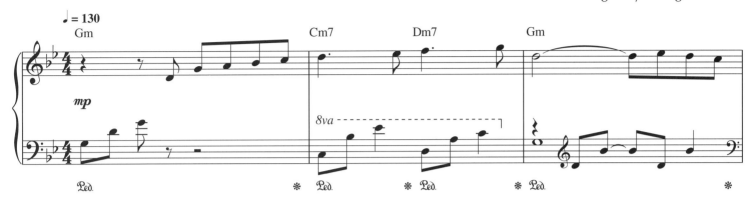

Pedal simile throughout

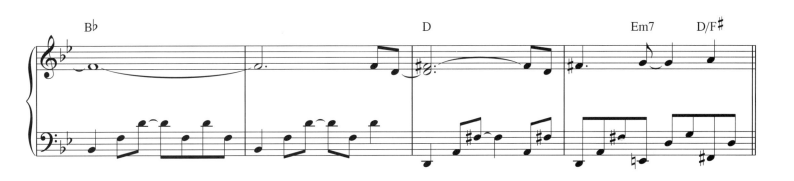

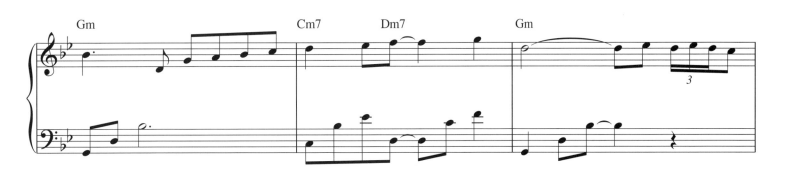

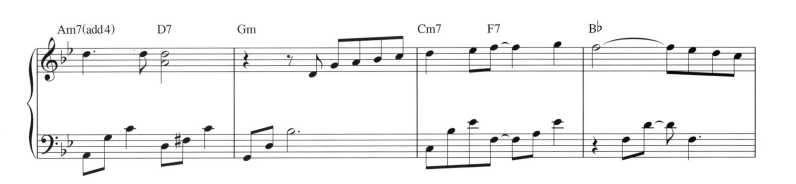

GRADUATION
from the solo piano album PLAINS

By GEORGE WINSTON

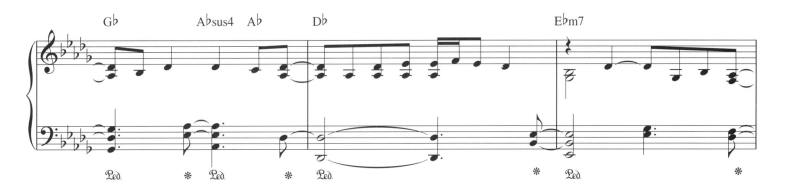

Pedal simile throughout

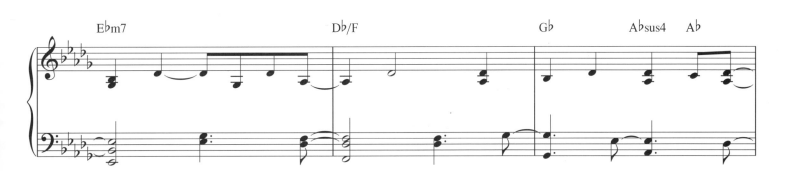

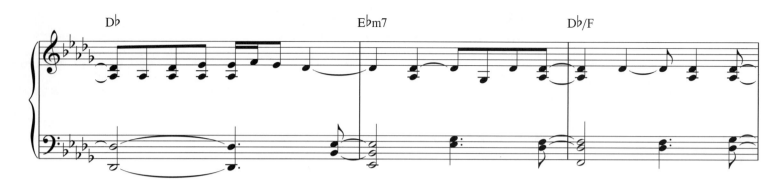

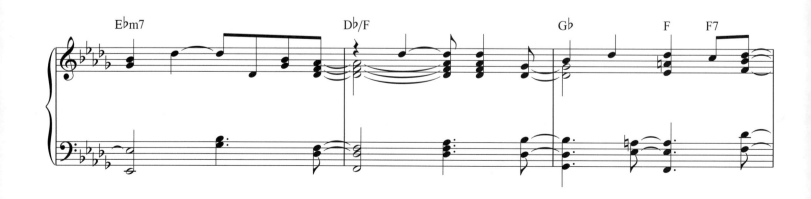

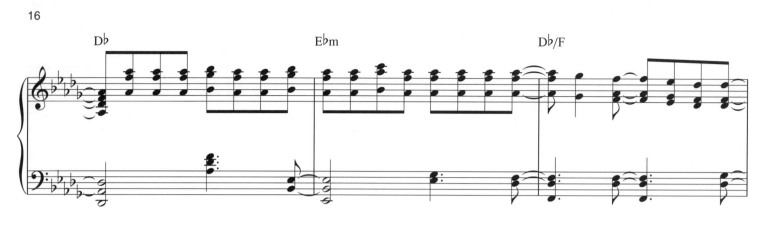

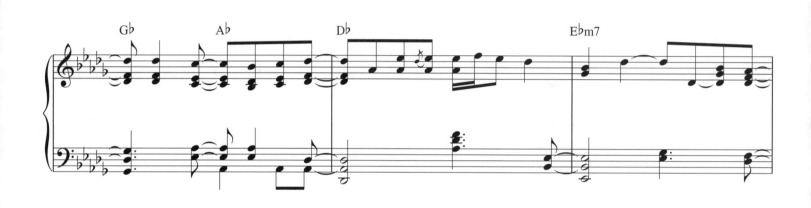

JOY
from the solo piano album DECEMBER

By J.S. BACH
Arranged by George Winston and David Qualey

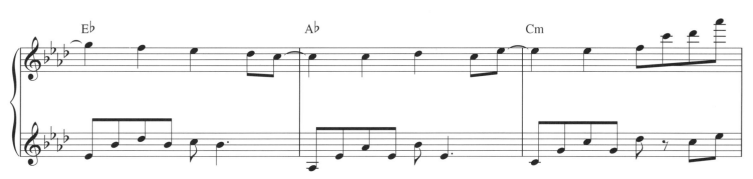

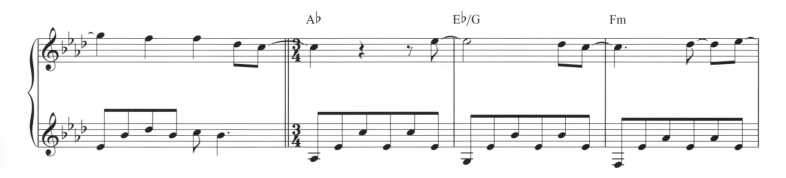

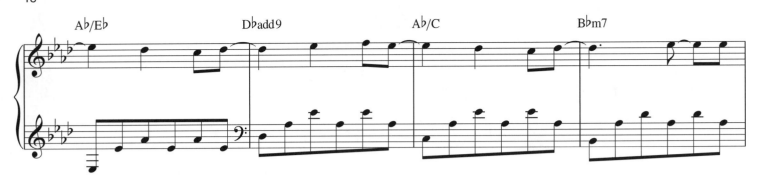

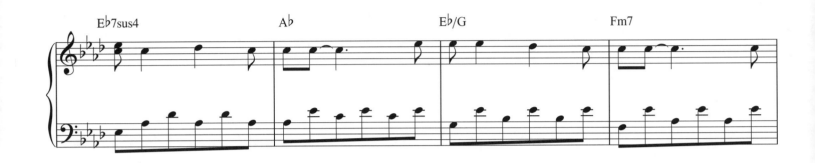

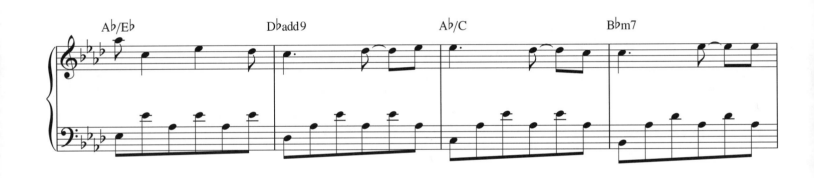

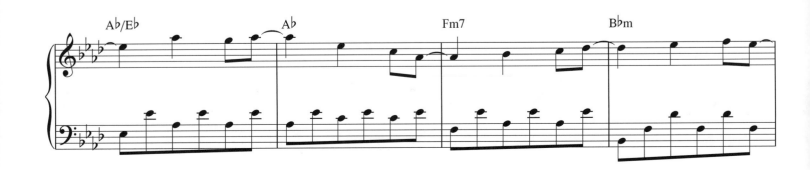

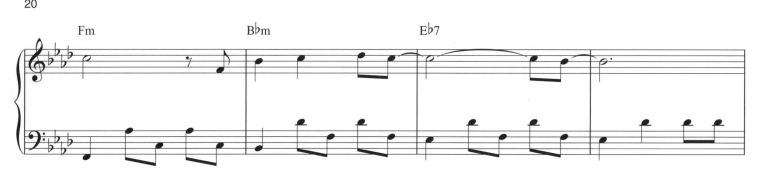

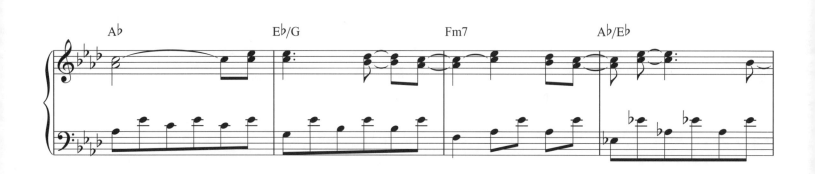

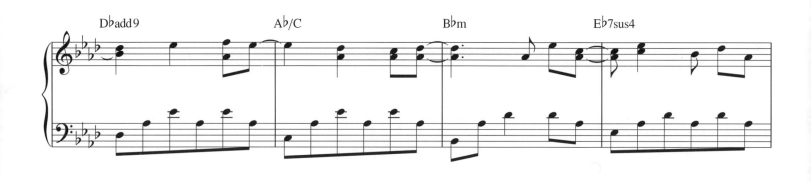

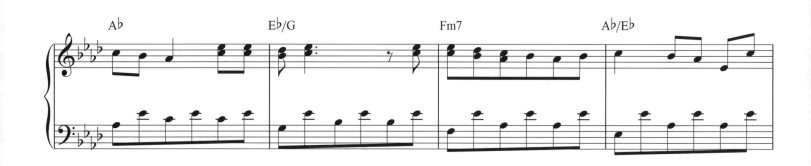

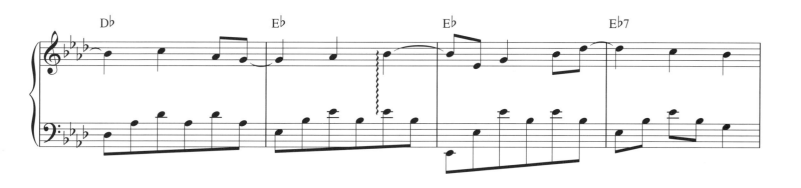

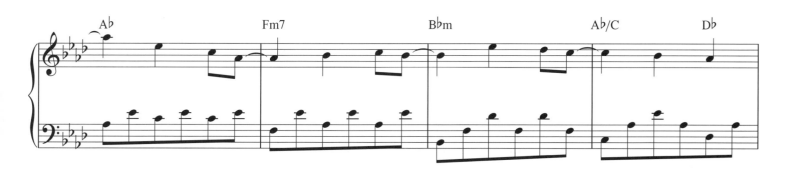

22

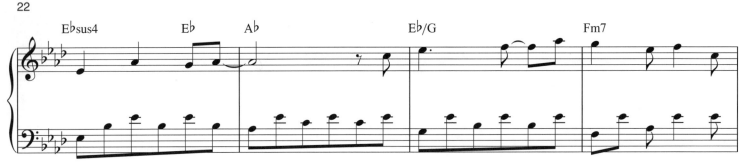

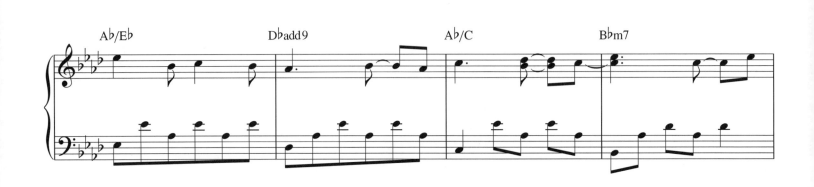

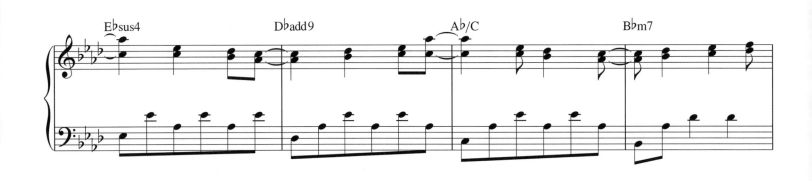

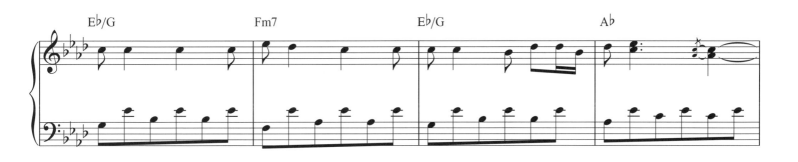

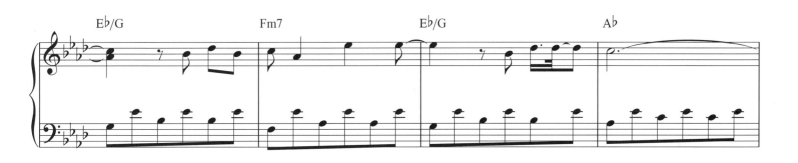

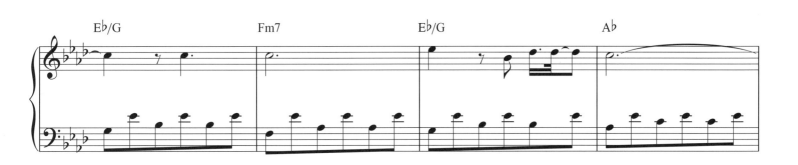

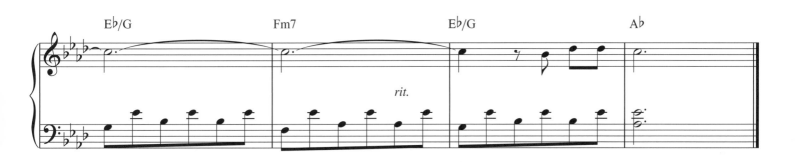

LORETA and DESIREE'S BOUQUET – PART I

from the solo piano album SUMMER

By GEORGE WINSTON

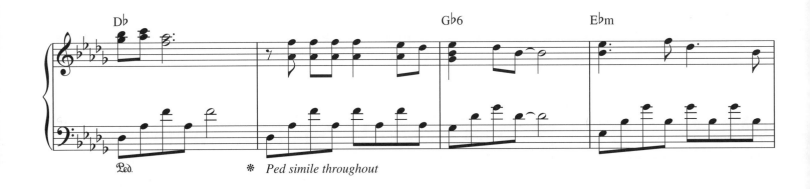

Ped simile throughout

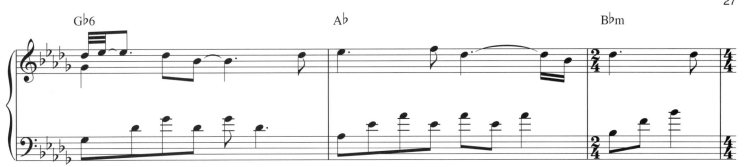

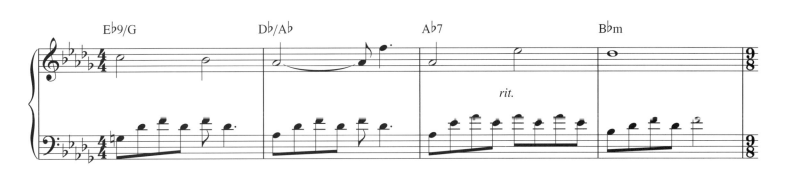

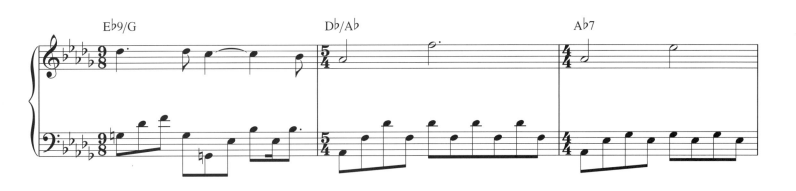

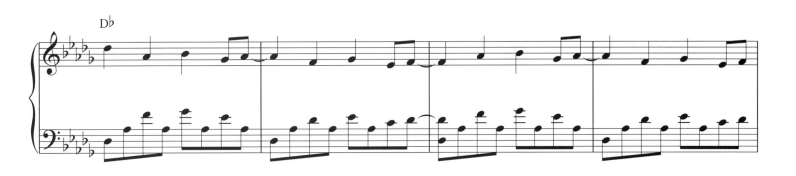

LONGING
from the solo piano album AUTUMN

By GEORGE WINSTON

Tempo di Rubato

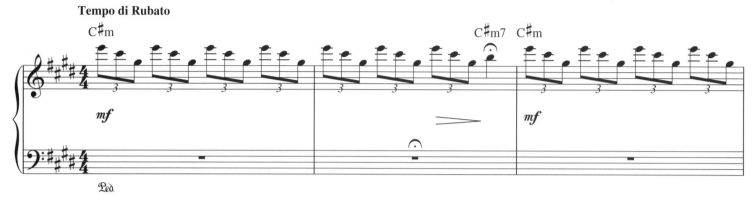

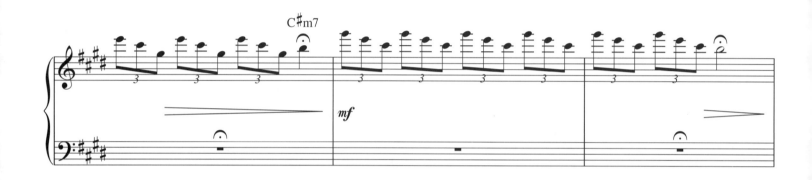

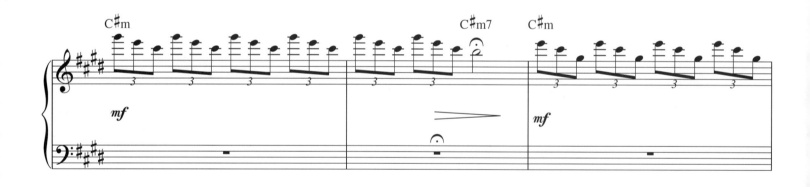

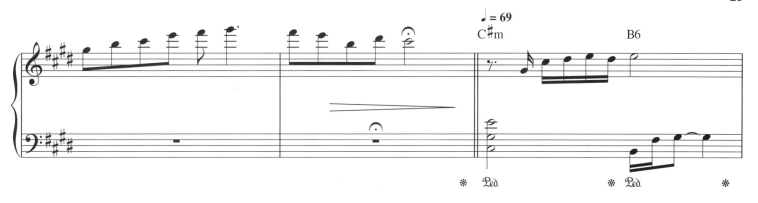

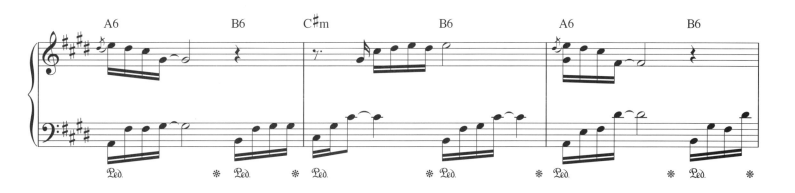

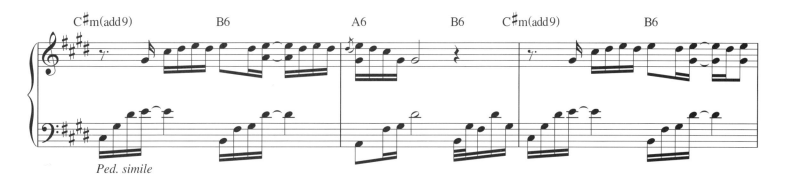

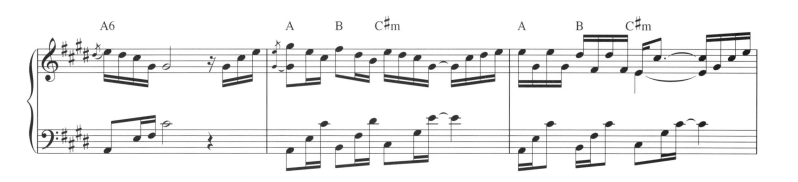

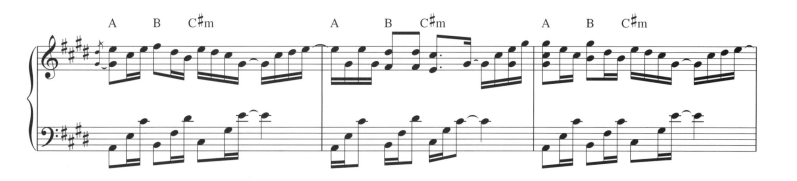

30

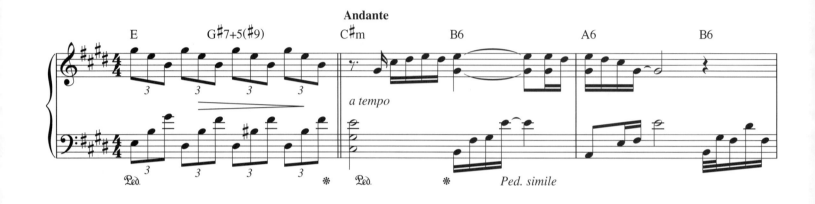

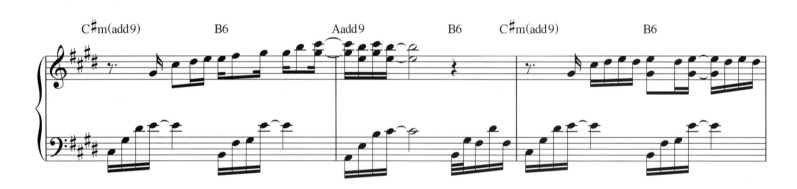

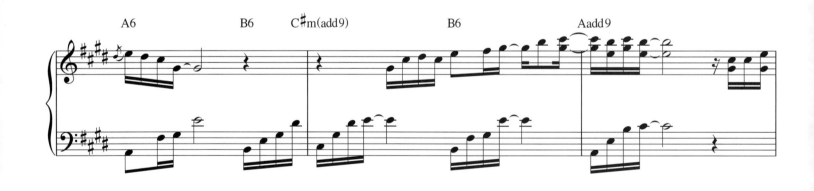

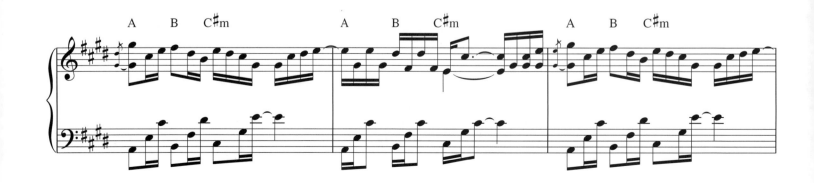

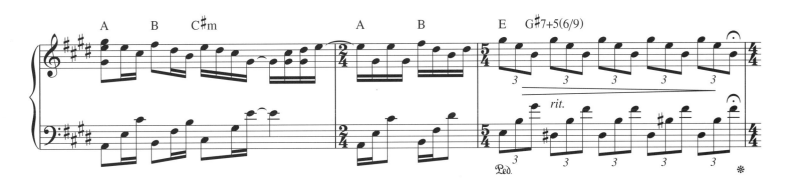

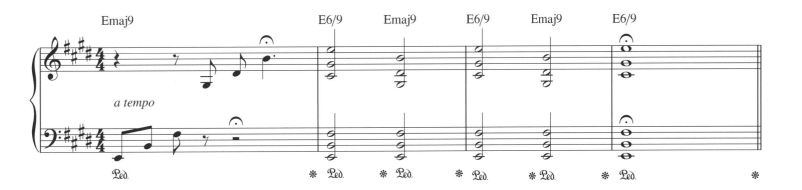

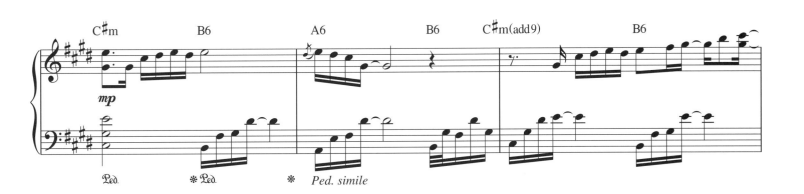

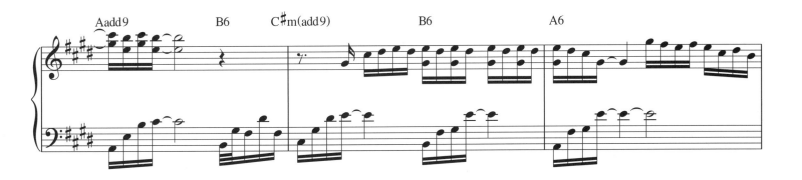

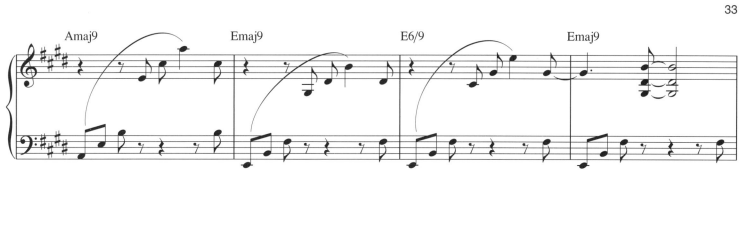

33

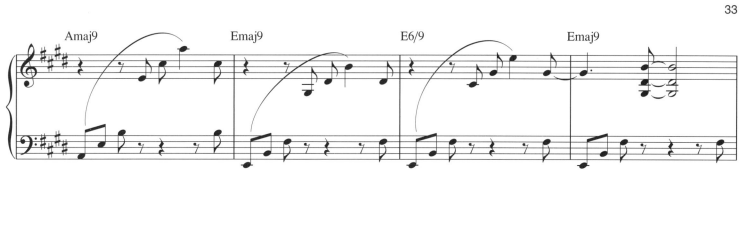

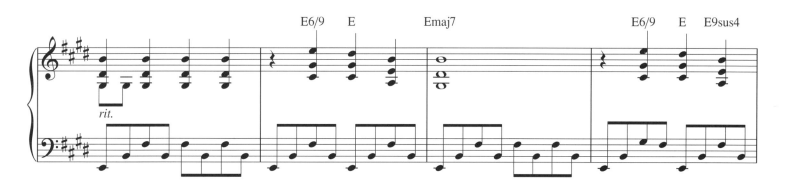

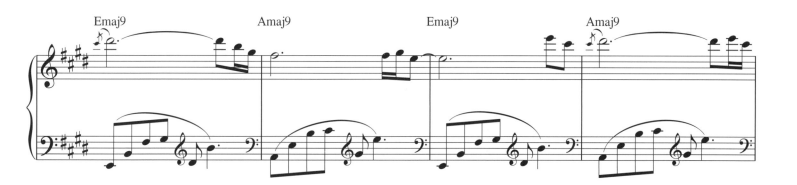

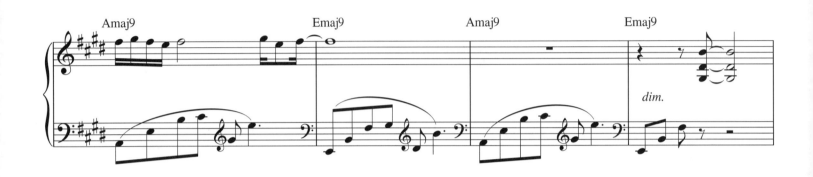

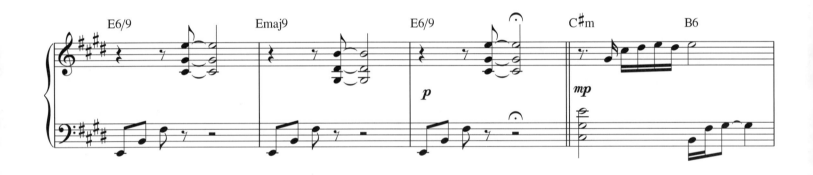

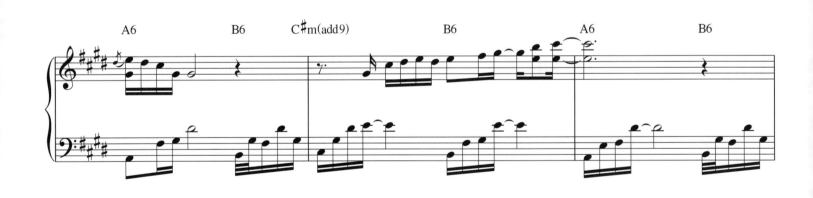

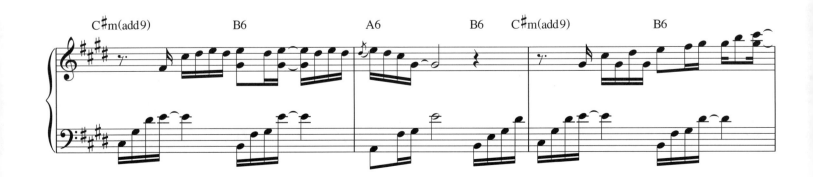

LULLABY
from the solo piano album SUMMER

By GEORGE WINSTON
Epilogue by Steve Ferguson

Pedal throughout

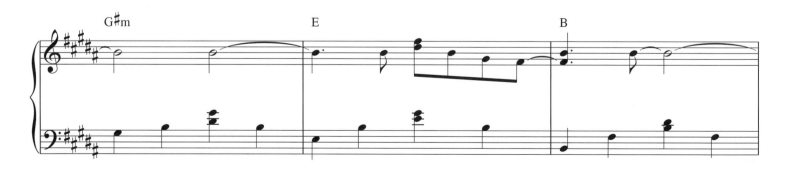

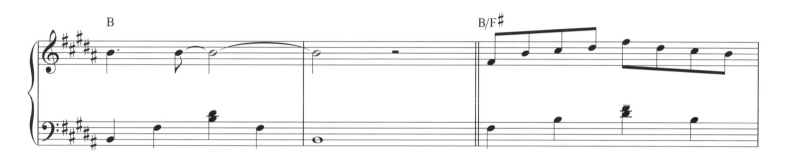

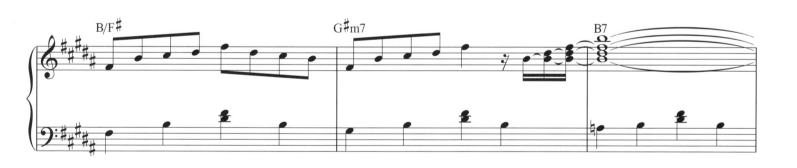

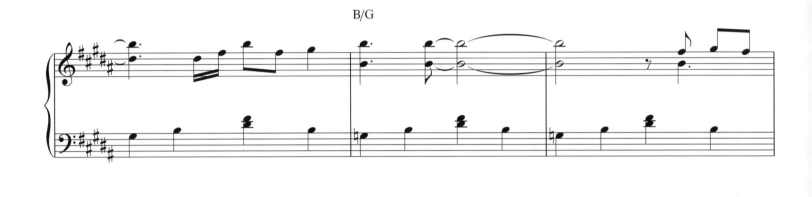

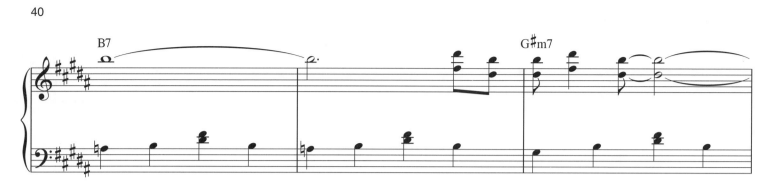

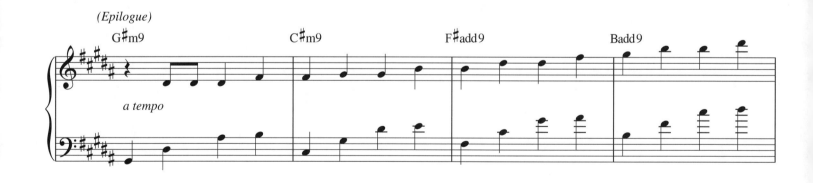

NEW HOPE BLUES
from the solo piano album BALLADS AND BLUES - 1972

By GEORGE WINSTON

Stride piano style (♩ = 225)

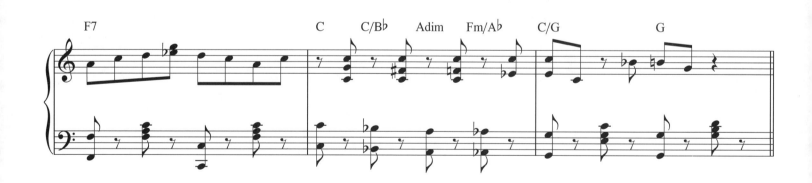

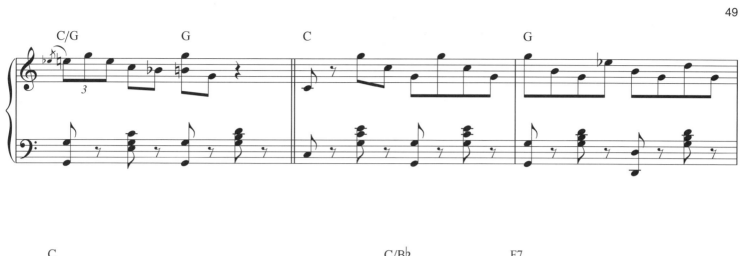

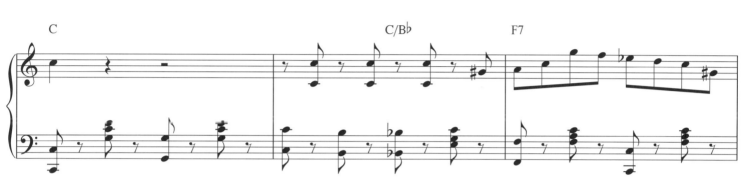

PRELUDE/CAROL OF THE BELLS
from the solo piano album DECEMBER

"Prelude" by GEORGE WINSTON
"Carol of the Bells" is traditional Ukrainian,
Arranged by George Winston

Prelude

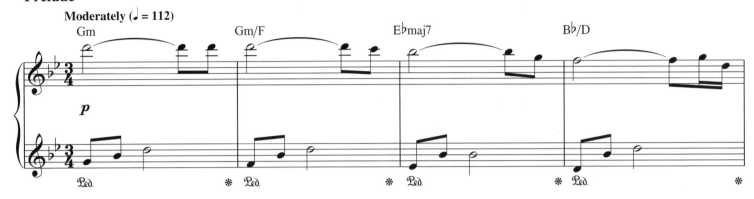

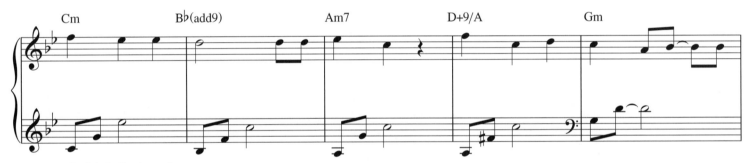

Pedal simile throughout

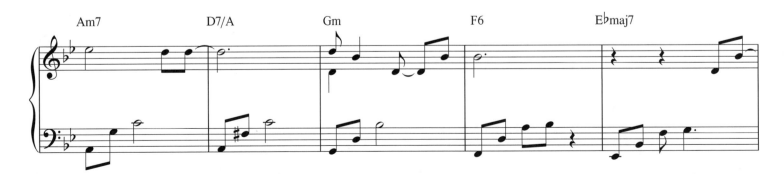

Carol of the Bells

Allegretto (♩ = 172)

REFLECTION
from the solo piano album WINTER INTO SPRING

By GEORGE WINSTON

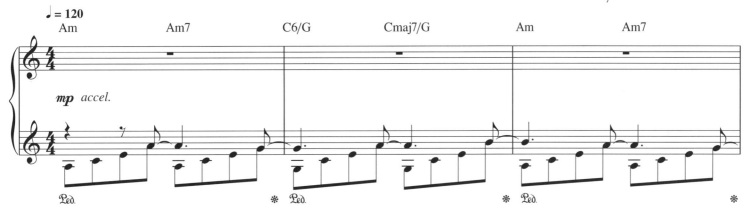

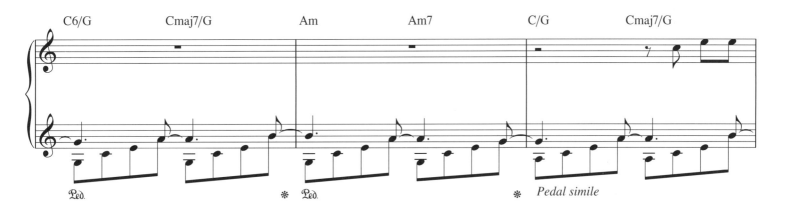

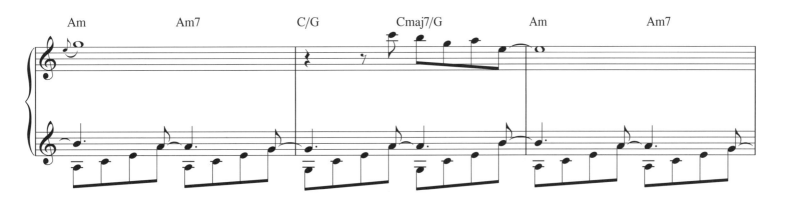

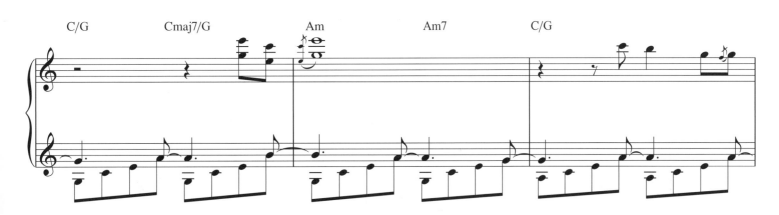

58

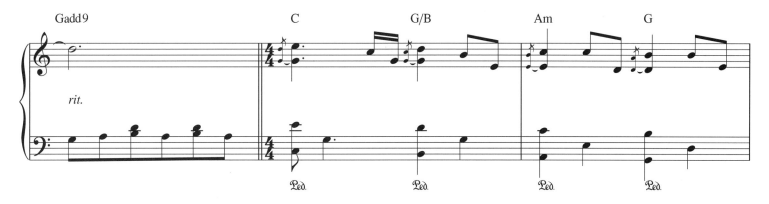

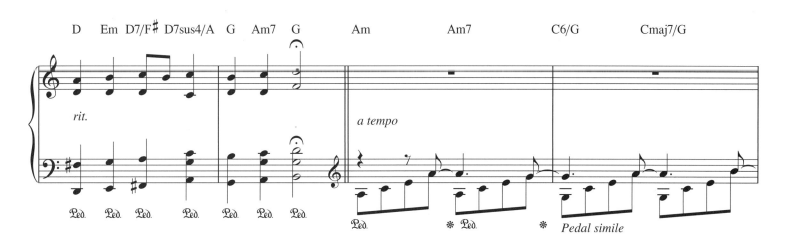

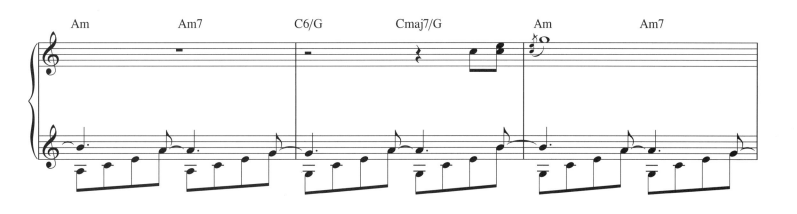

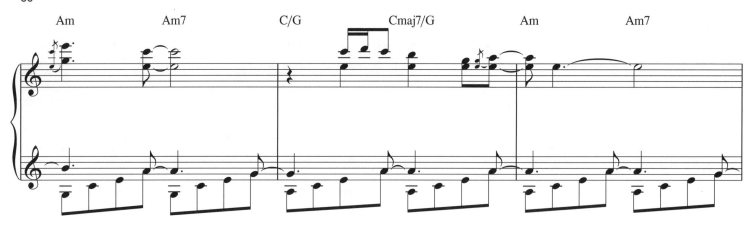

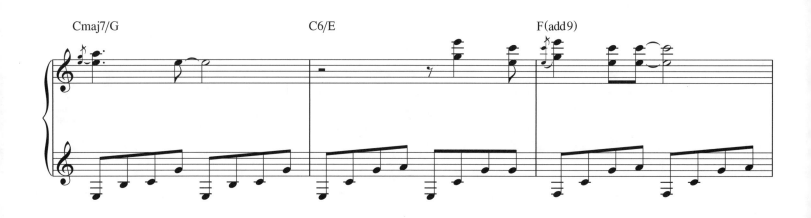

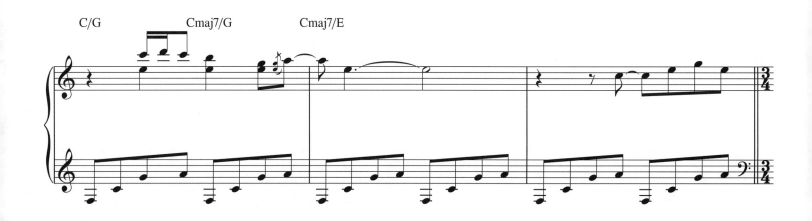

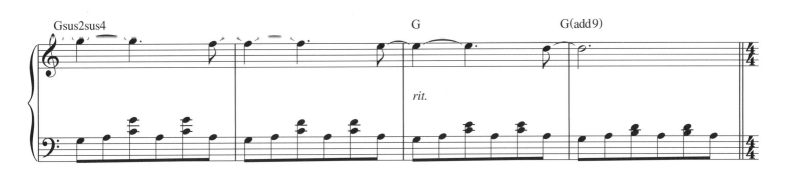

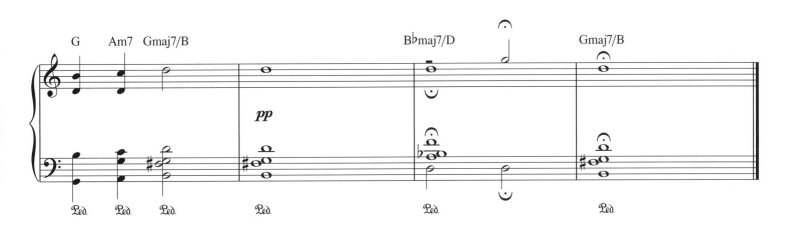

STEVENSON

from the solo piano album GULF COAST BLUES & IMPRESSIONS – A HURRICANE RELIEF BENEFIT

By GEORGE WINSTON

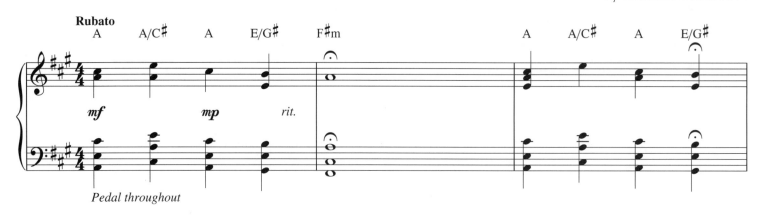

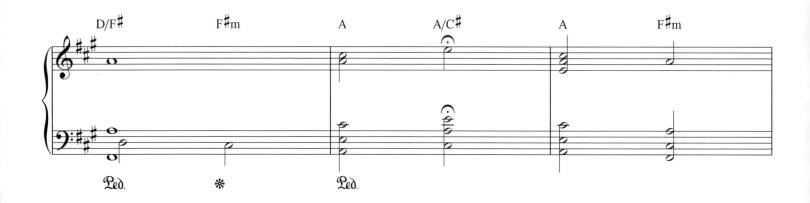

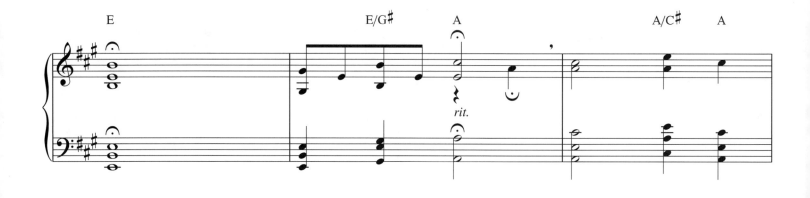

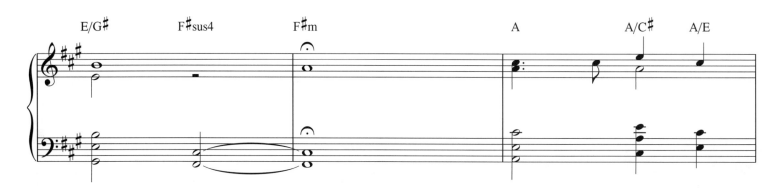

(Variations On)
BAMBOO
from the solo piano album MONTANA – A LOVE STORY

Traditional Chinese Lullaby
Arranged by George Winston

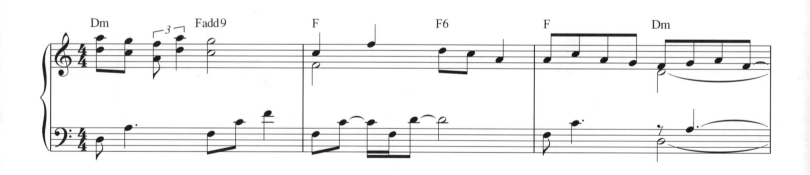

* *The bowing effect in line 3 measure 1, and line 5 measure 3, is achieved by slowly releasing the sustain pedal.*

THANKSGIVING
from the solo piano album DECEMBER

By GEORGE WINSTON

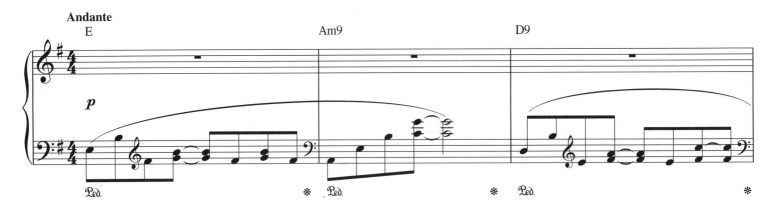

THUMBELINA
from the solo piano album MONTANA – A LOVE STORY

By MARK ISHAM
Arranged by George Winston

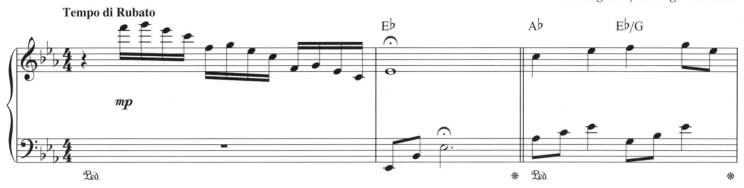

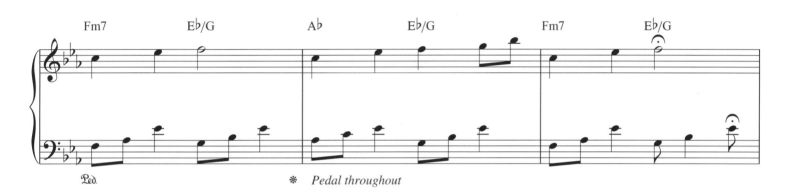

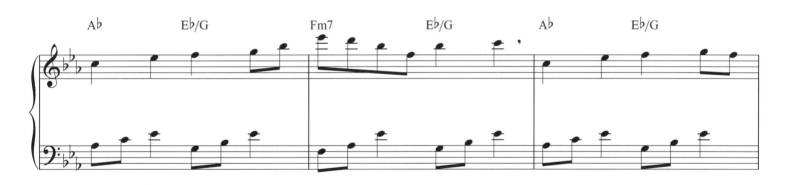

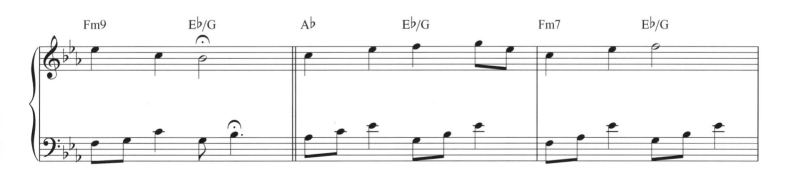

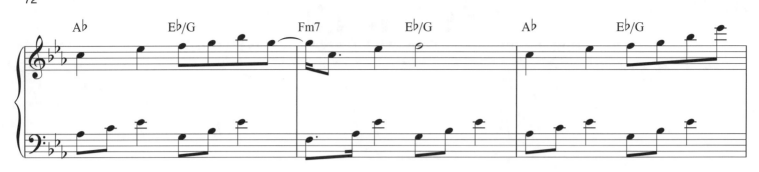

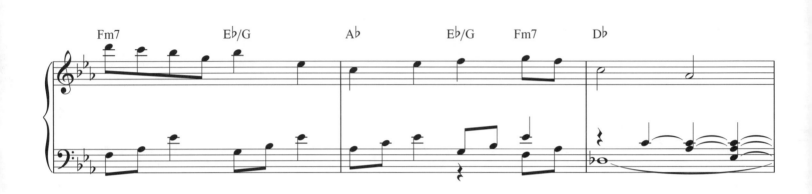

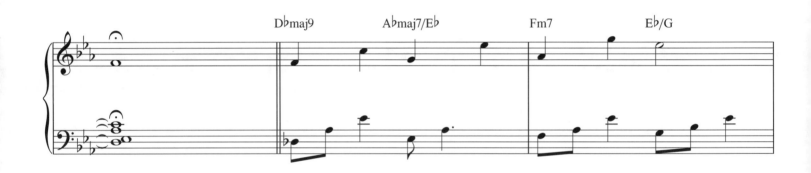

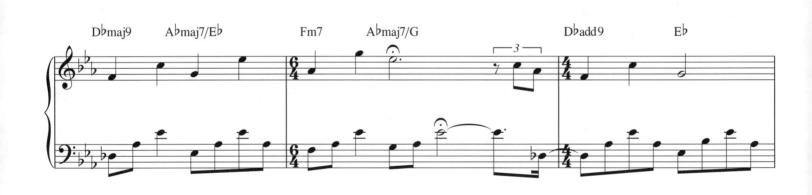

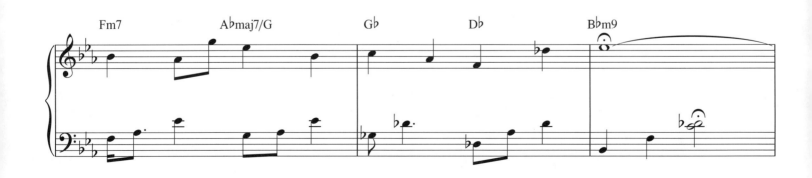

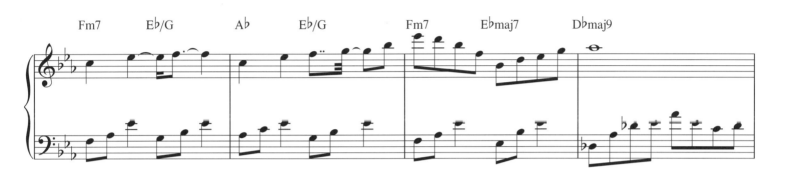

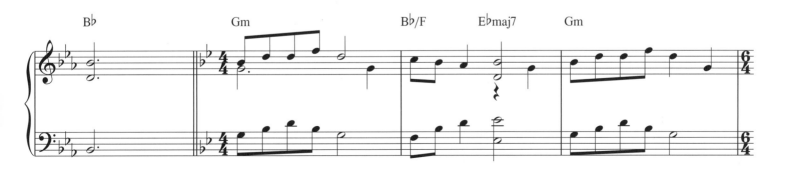

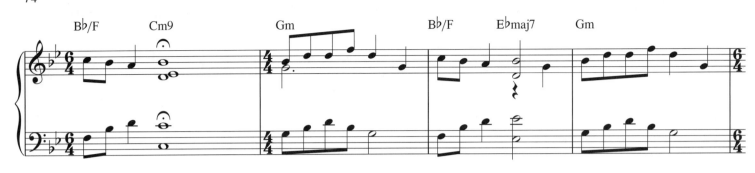

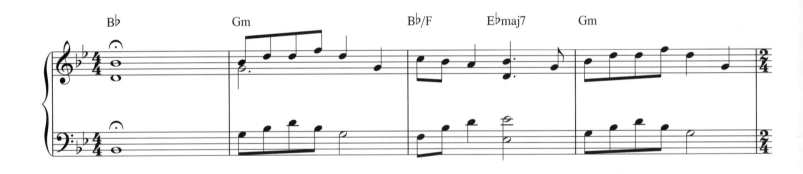

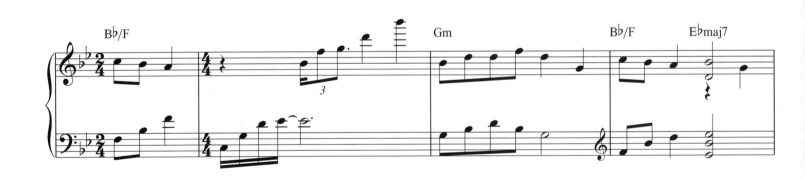

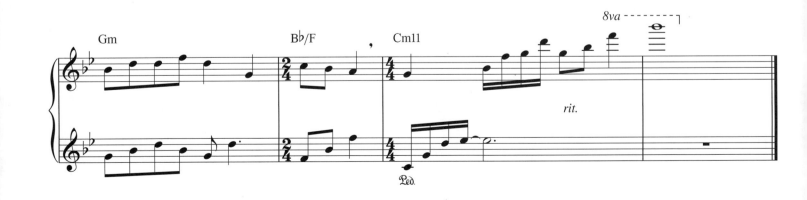

THE TWISTING OF THE HAY ROPE

from the solo piano album MONTANA – A LOVE STORY

Traditional Irish
Arranged by George Winston,
Patrick Ball and Tim Britton

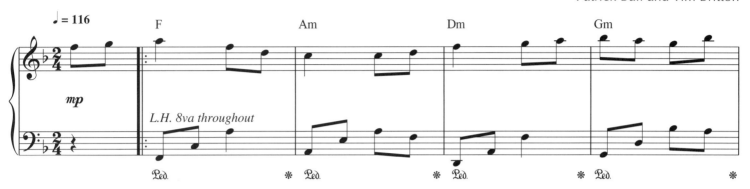

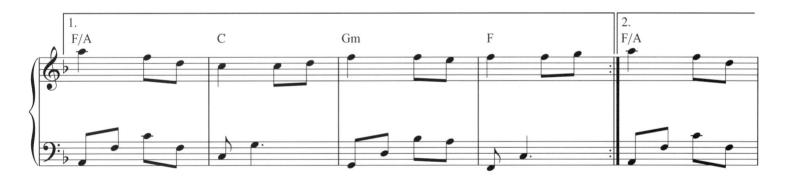

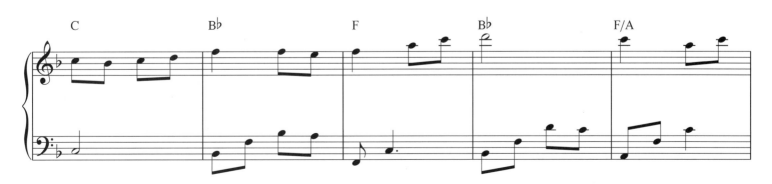

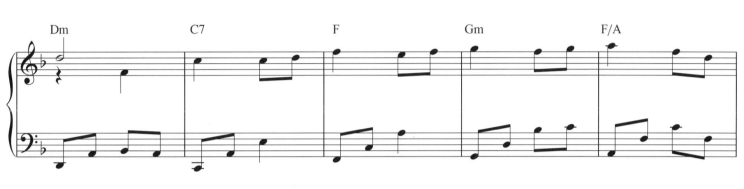

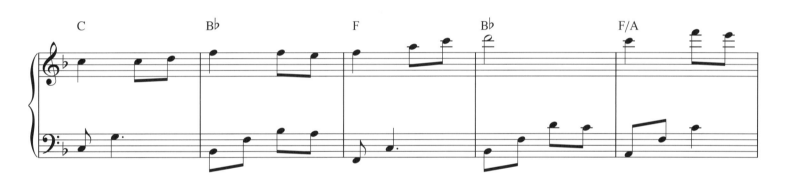

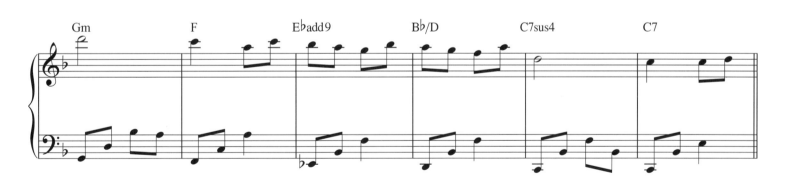

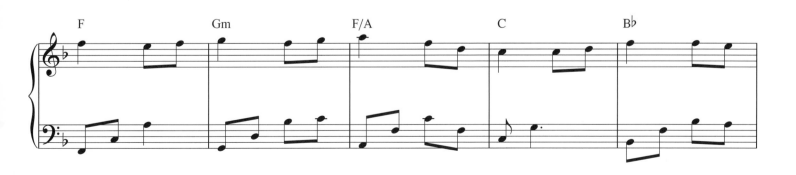

VARIATIONS ON THE KANON BY PACHELBEL

from the solo piano album DECEMBER

By JOHANN PACHELBEL
Arranged by George Winston

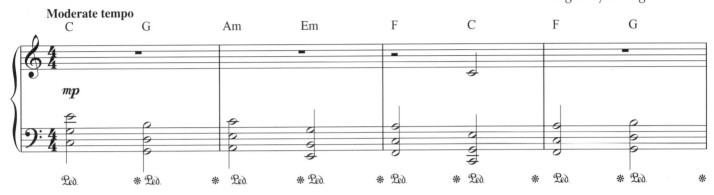

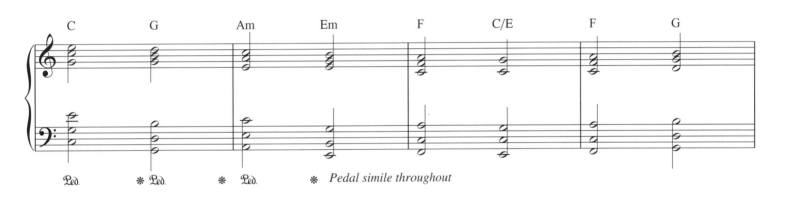

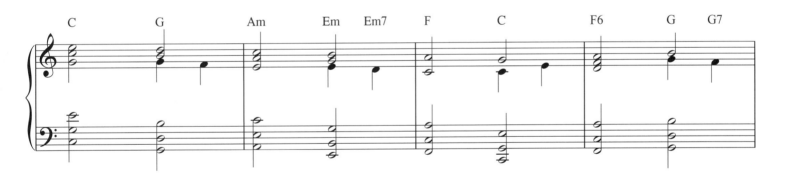

82

THE VELVETEEN RABBIT
from the soundtrack recording THE VELVETEEN RABBIT

By GEORGE WINSTON

86

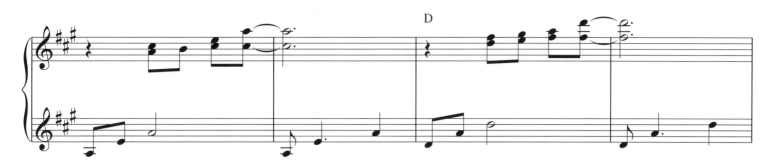

The Velveteen Rabbit

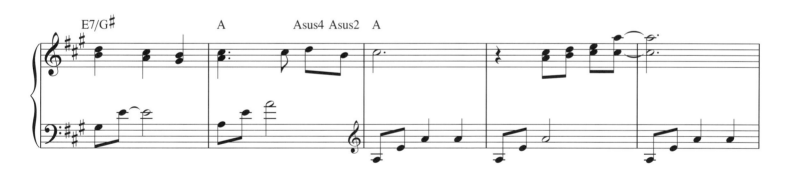

WALKING IN THE AIR
(excerpt)
from THE SNOWMAN
from the solo piano album FOREST

By HOWARD BLAKE

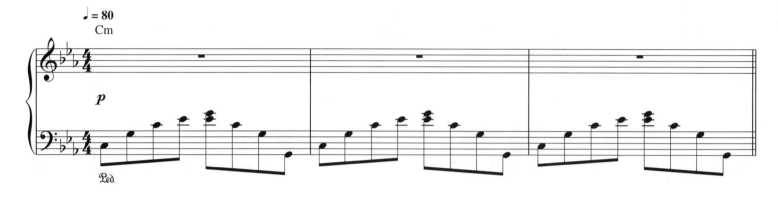

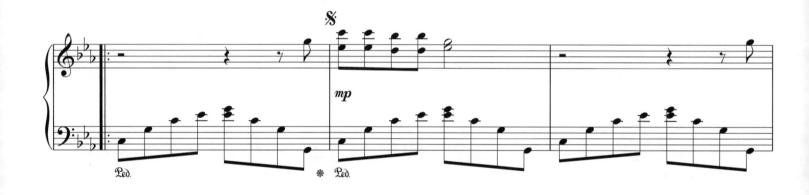

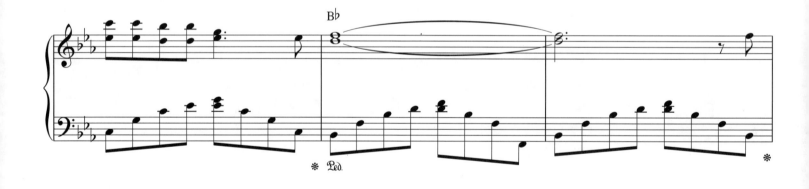

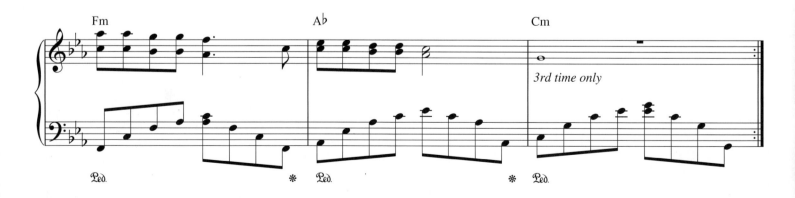

BUILDING THE SNOWMAN

from THE SNOWMAN
from the solo piano album FOREST

By HOWARD BLAKE

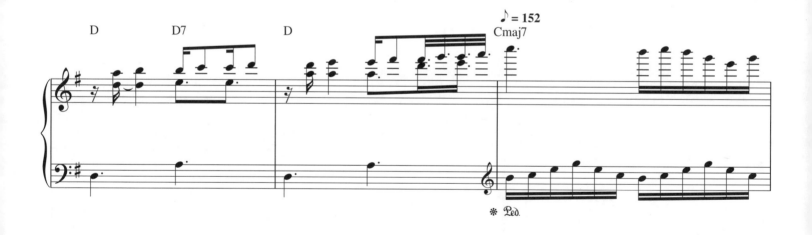

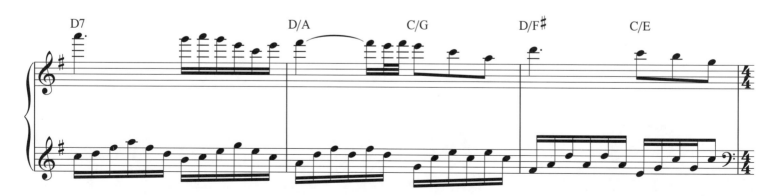

THE SNOWMAN'S MUSIC BOX DANCE

from THE SNOWMAN
from the solo piano album FOREST

By HOWARD BLAKE

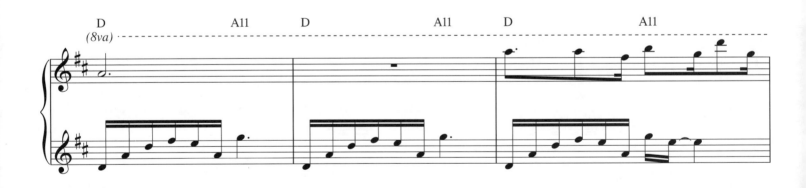

BIOGRAPHY

Born in 1949, George grew up mainly in Montana, and also spent his later formative years in Mississippi and Florida. During this time, his favorite music was instrumental rock and instrumental R&B, including Floyd Cramer, The Ventures, Booker T & The MG's, Jimmy Smith, and many more. Inspired by R&B, jazz, Blues, and rock (especially The Doors), George began playing organ in 1967. In 1971 he switched to the acoustic piano after hearing recordings from the 1920s and the 1930s by the legendary stride pianists Thomas "Fats" Waller and the late Teddy Wilson. In addition to working on stride piano, he also at this time came up with his own style of melodic instrumental music on solo piano, called folk piano. In 1972 he recorded his first solo piano album BALLADS AND BLUES 1972, for the late guitarist John Fahey's Takoma label.

His latest solo piano recording is GULF COAST BLUES & IMPRESSIONS—A HURRICANE RELIEF BENEFIT, released in 2006. This album has six compositions by George, and pieces by three great New Orleans pianists, Henry Butler, James Booker, and Dr. John, as well as George's arrangement of the traditional *When the Saints Go Marching In.*

Since 1980 George has released nine other solo piano albums: AUTUMN (1980); WINTER INTO SPRING (1982); DECEMBER (1982); SUMMER (1991); FOREST (1994); LINUS & LUCY—THE MUSIC OF VINCE GUARALDI (1996), which features compositions by the late jazz pianist, including *Cast Your Fate to the Wind* and pieces from the Peanuts® TV specials; PLAINS (1999), which was inspired by his Eastern Montana upbringing; NIGHT DIVIDES THE DAY—THE MUSIC OF THE DOORS (2002); and MONTANA—A LOVE STORY (2004).

Also, in November 2001 George released REMEMBRANCE—A MEMORIAL BENEFIT, a six song CD of piano, guitar, and harmonica solos, to benefit those affected by 9/11. He has also worked with the late George Levenson of Informed Democracy (**www.informeddemocracy.com**) on three projects: a solo guitar soundtrack for SADAKO AND THE THOUSAND PAPER CRANES, and soundtracks of piano, guitar and harmonica solos for PUMPKIN CIRCLE, and BREAD COMES TO LIFE. In 1984 he also did the solo piano soundtrack for the children's story THE VELVETEEN RABBIT for Rabbit Ears Productions.

The piano music George is currently working on is about two-thirds New Orleans R&B oriented, and about one-third melodic music played in his folk piano style.

He is also presently concentrating on live performances and is studying the playing of the great New Orleans pianists Henry Butler, the late James Booker, the late Professor Longhair, Dr. John, and Jon Cleary. He is also working on interpreting pieces on solo piano by his favorite composers, including Vince Guaraldi, Professor Longhair, The Doors, Frank Zappa, Randy Newman, Sam Cooke, Ray Charles, Curtis Mayfield, Al Kooper, Laura Nyro, Bob Dylan, Dr. John, Henry Butler, James Booker, Jon Cleary, John Coltrane, Milt Jackson, John Hartford, Taj Mahal, Bruce Cockburn, Philip Aaberg, and others, to play at concerts, and at his solo piano dances where he features R&B, slow dance songs, and more.

Most of the time George is touring, playing solo piano concerts (the *Summer Show* or the *Winter Show*), solo guitar concerts, solo harmonica concerts, and solo piano dances.

George is also working on solo guitar and is recording the masters of the Hawaiian Slack Key guitar for an extensive series of albums for Dancing Cat Records (**www.dancingcat.com**). Slack Key is the name for the beautiful solo fingerstyle guitar tradition unique to Hawai'i (which began in the early 1800s and predated the steel guitar by over half a century).

George Winston plays Steinway Pianos

www.georgewinston.com

SELECTED DISCOGRAPHY

SOLO PIANO ALBUMS

GULF COAST BLUES & IMPRESSIONS—A HURRICANE RELIEF BENEFIT – includes *Stevenson*

MONTANA—A LOVE STORY – includes *The Twisting of the Hay Rope*, *Thumbelina*, and *(Variations On) Bamboo*

NIGHT DIVIDES THE DAY—THE MUSIC OF THE DOORS

REMEMBRANCE—A MEMORIAL BENEFIT – six song CD, with piano, guitar, and harmonica solos, benefiting those affected by 9/11.

PLAINS – includes *Graduation*

LINUS & LUCY—THE MUSIC OF VINCE GUARALDI

FOREST – includes *The Cradle*; and from **The Snowman**: *Walking in the Air*, *Building the Snowman*, and *The Snowman's Music Box Dance*

SUMMER – special enhanced edition, with one bonus track – includes *Black Stallion*, *Loreta and Desiree's Bouquet—Part 1*, and *Lullaby*

DECEMBER – 20th Anniversary enhanced edition, with two bonus tracks – includes *Joy*, *Prelude/Carol of the Bells*, *Thanksgiving*, and V*ariations on the Kanon by Pachelbel*

WINTER INTO SPRING – 20th Anniversary enhanced edition, with one bonus track – includes *Reflection*

AUTUMN – 20th Anniversary enhanced edition, with one bonus track – includes *Longing*

BALLADS AND BLUES 1972 – 20th Anniversary enhanced edition, with five bonus tracks – includes *New Hope Blues*

SOUNDTRACKS

THE VELVETEEN RABBIT – Solo piano soundtrack accompanying narration by Meryl Streep, for the classic children's story written by Margery Williams in 1922 – 20th Anniversary enhanced edition, with the piano solos alone released for the first time, along with a bonus track. Produced by Rabbit Ears Productions, and also released on DVD by Sony, and as book/audio CD set available at Starbucks. Also see **www.rabbitears.com** and **www.greattapes.com/gt/series.phtml/rabbitears** - includes the song *The Velveteen Rabbit*

SADAKO AND THE THOUSAND PAPER CRANES – Based on the true story of Sadako Sasaki, a young Japanese girl in post-WWII Hiroshima, who became a contemporary heroine of peace. Solo guitar soundtrack accompanying narration by Liv Ullman on Part 1, with the guitar solos alone on Part 2. Video available from Informed Democracy (1-800-827 0949). Also see **www.sadako.com** and **www.informeddemocracy.com**.

PUMPKIN CIRCLE – An entertaining and educational children's story about the growth of pumpkins through the cycle of the seasons. Solo piano, guitar, and harmonica soundtrack accompanying narration by Danny Glover. Video only, available from Informed Democracy. Also see **www.pumpkincircle.com** and **www.informeddemocracy.com**

BREAD COMES TO LIFE – The story of making bread from a garden of wheat to a loaf to eat. Solo piano, guitar, and harmonica soundtrack accompanying narration by Lily Tomlin. Video only, available from Informed Democracy. Also see **www.breadcomestolife.com** and **www.informeddemocracy.com**

THIS IS AMERICA, CHARLIE BROWN, VOLUME 6: THE BIRTH OF THE CONSTITUTION – Piano and harpsichord solos, playing mainly the late Vince Guaraldi's compositions, accompanying the narration. Video only.

For a complete discography and more information see **www.georgewinston.com**